LESLEY M. KAYE

Art with the Universe

MY COSMIC CANVAS

Channeling for a new understanding
of your life and ways, and the truth of reality

All rights reserved; no part of this book may be reproduced, stored in a retrieval system, or transmitted, in any form or by any means, without the prior permission in writing from the publisher, nor be otherwise circulated in any form of binding or cover other than that in which it is published and without a similar condition, including this condition being imposed on the subsequent purchaser.

First published in Great Britain in 2023 by Quill Literature

Copyright © 2023 by Lesley M. Kaye
Editorial Services by Marsha D. Phillips
Cover Design and Typesetting by Arjan van Woensel

ISBN: 978-1-7397426-1-4

The moral right of the authors has been asserted.

Nothing in this book is to be taken as professional medical advice and is the opinion and experience of the authors. The authors and publisher accept no liability for damage of any nature resulting directly or indirectly from the application or use of any information contained within this book. Any information acted upon from this book is at the reader's sole discretion and risk.

First Edition

I dedicate this book to you, divine channel to the wonders of the Universe. May the time creating your inspired art be one of heartfelt love and joy.

INTRODUCTION

Welcome to *Art with the Universe: My Cosmic Canvas*, a companion to *Diary of a Scribe to the Universe: A Cosmic Accord*. May these pages be filled with your divinely inspired art and ignite an exciting journey of inward discovery for you!

Channelling can take many forms. Writing, drawing, meditating, creating and listening to music are just a few ways inspiration is awakened. When channelling art, freely use any colours and draw any shapes or images that come to mind.

Relax. This is not an art course. Anything you create is perfect in its own right. If the process feels strange at first, don't worry, with time it will feel more natural and rewarding. You may find that your ability to see images or designs is affected by how you feel, what's on your mind, or things you need to do. Put away your 'to-do list' and dedicate just 5–10 minutes to yourself and your channelling. Relax and allow the energy to flow. You will likely find the experience improves as you develop this creative habit.

Below are additional tips to help you move into this wonderful experience.

****

The Ritual of Channelling

****

When

Set aside time to channel, in the morning or evening - whenever feels best for you - the choice is yours and will depend on how you feel at certain times of the day and your daily commitments. If possible, select a time you will not be disturbed by others or your phone, or have other possible interruptions.

Where

Find an area that is dedicated to channelling your art. If you don't have one at present, create one. If that isn't possible, make sure you feel comfortable where you choose to create your art.

How

I have found that the first and best approach to channelling art is to relax. Choose an activity that brings you calm and peace of mind, such as lighting a candle and observing the flame, playing gentle music, spending time in nature, or meditating. It may also help to imagine yourself in a large bubble of light. I like white light, generally, but let the right colour come to you. Take 3 deep breaths. This is your signal to spirit that you would like to make contact. Don't forget to keep taking nice deep, relaxed breaths. When you feel relaxed, choose your medium: pencils, inks, gel pens, markers, paints - gather any materials you like to use. You do not need to spend a lot on art supplies. Pencils, markers and gel pens are inexpensive and may be items you already have at home.

In subsequent pages, you will find three designs I have created to illustrate how inspired art may appear as your imagination begins to flow. However you feel inspired to create your art is perfect, just as the results will be, and you may be drawn to use different mediums at different times; again, this is perfect.

Not all my designs are created in one sitting, though this can happen. Often a design is created in stages, perhaps weeks apart, when I feel moved to continue and I can see the image more clearly in my mind. Often, whilst creating a design, I will feel the urge to draw certain shapes or lines and use specific colours. Again, this is my personal experience; it is not intended to show you how you should or must create your art. Whatever form your message comes in, it is perfect! The most important thing is to enjoy the experience. This is a special communication just for you, so do what feels right, what brings you happiness.

Don't forget to look at the companion publications in the Lesley M. Kaye with Yahvay collection:

Diary of a Scribe to the Universe: A Cosmic Accord
On This Day of Days: Daily Messages of Love and Wisdom
Chatting with the Universe: My Cosmic Diary
Journalling with the Universe: My Divine Conversations (unlined)
Let Your Sparkle Sparkle: Ponder and Power Cards
Let Your Sparkle Sparkle: Desk Calendar

Further details for these publications can be found at www.quill-literature.co.uk

By far, the most important thing is to enjoy the process. Have fun!

Lesley

This gel pen design shows how a simple image can be striking.

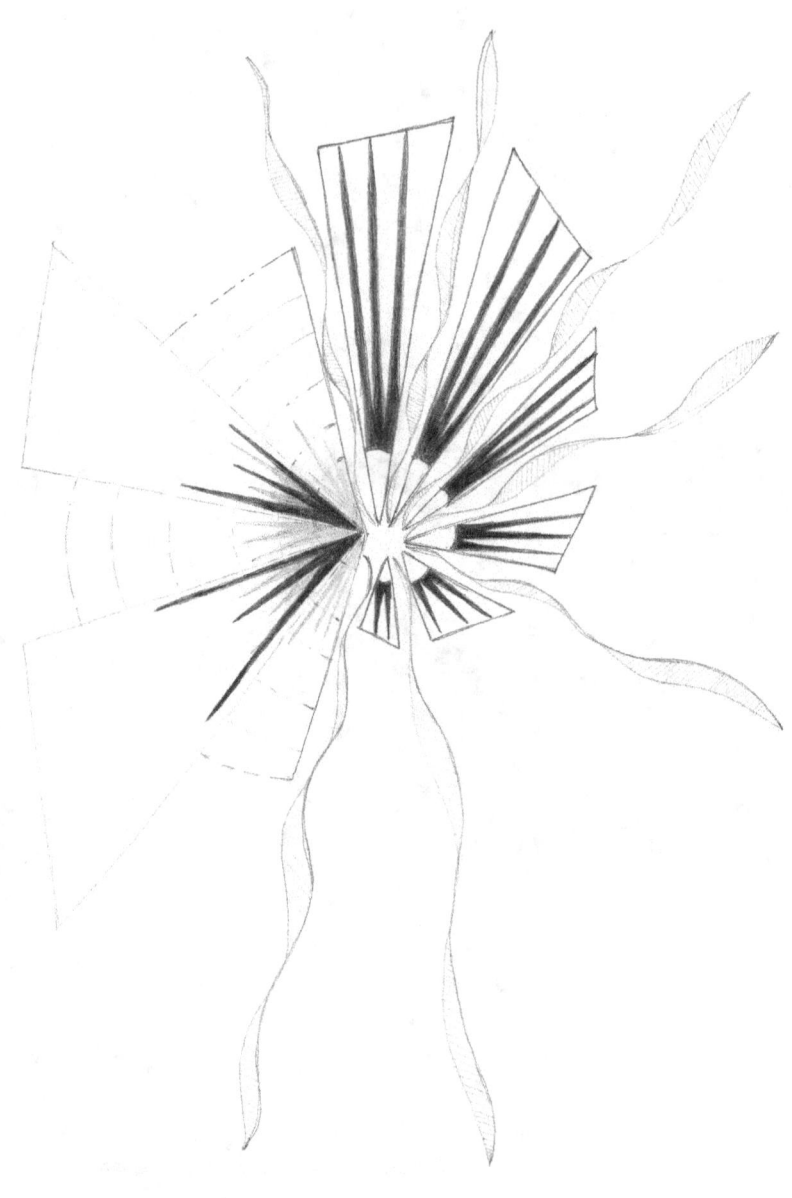

Pencil drawings allow for various degrees of shading, enhanced by the effects of simple lines and an eraser.

Design using black and white acrylic paints and art spatula on heavy-weight paper.

About Lesley M. Kaye

Having spent most of her working life in education, Lesley is now semi-retired apart from teaching some Italian. She lives in England with her family and three rescue cats. Along with a passion for channelling and all things spiritual, Lesley also loves nature, languages, art, crystals, music, property programmes and reading.

Channelling has now become a wonderful way of life for Lesley. This passion extends to encouraging others to channel for themselves to discover the love and wisdom of the Universe on their own personal journey.

www.ingramcontent.com/pod-product-compliance
Lightning Source LLC
Chambersburg PA
CBHW072053110526
44590CB00018B/3152